Water Garden Lifestyles

EXPLORING WATER FEATURES ACROSS NORTH AMERICA

water garden LIFESTYLES

EXPLORING WATER FEATURES ACROSS NORTH AMERICA

AQUASCAPE LIFESTYLES BOOKS

Published by

Aquascape Lifestyles Books

PO Box 638

West Chicago, IL 60186

877-206-7035

www.aquascapelifestyles.com

Jacket and book design by MMG

Printed in Korea

10 9 8 7 6 5 4 3 2 1

ISBN 0-9723214-4-6

CONTENTS

My Water Garden Journey

EVERYBODY WANTS A POND, MOST PEOPLE JUST DON'T KNOW IT … YET!
AND THAT'S WHY *WATER GARDEN LIFESTYLES* WAS CREATED – TO SHOW THE
WORLD THE BEAUTY, TRANQUILITY, AND PURE JOY THAT WATER GARDENS
bring to more and more people each year. For those who have already been
bitten by the "Water Gardening Bug," let this book be your inspiration to con-
tinue adapting, creating, and growing your own water feature – a never-end-
ing journey in itself.

My own water feature, pictured here, is a testament to that journey.
When I built my first pond to house my pet turtles in 1982, I used traditional
construction materials to create my backyard habitat. Little did I know that
concrete cracks, in-pond filters clog, and turtles are classic escape artists!

My journey in water gardening was, unfortunately, a common one. Because of problems like these, water gardening has gotten a bad rap as being
a high-maintenance, troublesome hobby – not one for the time-crunched
workaholic who personifies our modern era. And it's the time-crunched
workaholics who most need a water feature and all that comes with it!

Having "been there and done that," I set out to change the negative
image of water features and to shatter the stereotypes that accompany the
hobby by launching Aquascape Designs Inc., now North America's largest
water garden systems company.

The common theme you'll see throughout this book is that every water
feature pictured in these pages was built using the Aquascape Designs Ecosystem as its foundation. These water gardens are not only beautiful and low

ABOVE AND LEFT»
From a boy with a
dream for his turtles,
to a grown man with
a dream for a water
garden in everyone's
backyard, so they too
can experience an
aquatic paradise.

vii

maintenance, but they destroy the myths that "tradition-
ally" built ponds are based on – namely working *against*
Mother Nature. Aquascape Designs ponds are environ-
mentally friendly, beautiful, and low maintenance because
they do the opposite – they work *with* Mother Nature!

viii

The water gardening journey has other "constants"
besides the belief that everybody wants a pond and just
doesn't know it. Namely, no pond is too big, and a well-
designed water garden is never really complete.

My personal water garden is an acre in total area,
13 feet deep, has a cave for swimming (or scuba diving)
through, and besides being home to traditional koi, is
stocked with bass, bluegill, walleye, catfish, and crappie
(catch and release, of course) and guess what? I'm still
working on it! I just added a Pondless® Waterfall to the
front yard and I'm looking to totally replant my bog area
(there are just too many cool bog plants to not try some
new ones!).

And you know what? If I did finally achieve perfec-
tion, I'd have to buy a new house to build a new pond,

LEFT» Water gardens bring family members outdoors, together. Carla, Blake, and Ryan Wittstock are proof of this. LEFT CENTER» While this water feature is large by most people's standards, the enjoyment of having your own pond is immeasurable.

ix

because once you've been bitten by that "Water Gardening Bug," you'll not only be drawn out of your house to sit by your pond instead of the TV, but more often than not you'll be in it as well!

Here's to your own personal water gardening journey. I hope it's as rewarding as mine, and the hundreds of thousands who have discovered the Aquascape "lifestyle" as well. Let this book, our quarterly magazine, *Aquascape Lifestyles*, our water garden book, *The Ecosystem Pond*, and the North American Water Gardening Society be your inspiration into this wonderful hobby of water gardening.

From one pond lover to another … rock on!

Greg Wittstock

The Pond Guy™

1

THE WONDERFUL WORLD OF WATER GARDENING

SO YOU'VE JUST STEPPED OUT OF THE MUNDANE, EVERYDAY, REAL

WORLD – A PLACE THAT'S CHARACTERIZED BY STRIP MALLS, GAS STATIONS, OFFICE BUILDINGS, INTERSTATE HIGHWAYS, COMPUTERS, FAX MACHINES, television sets, and many more dubious distractions. You've now entered the wonderful world of water gardening! Congratulations, you're going to love it.

But here's a fair warning. You may feel a little like Alice after she dove into the rabbit hole because, in this book you're going to discover miraculous things like crystal-clear water cascading over waterfalls into meandering streams and eventually into ponds that are loaded with colorful koi and goldfish, as well as beautiful and aromatic plants … a world where everything is totally natural. Best of all, this aquatic paradise is something that, if you don't already, you can have in your own backyard.

In this book, you'll discover marvelous photos taken by many backyard "ponderers" who, just like you, love ponds and happened to find themselves in the right place at the right moment, with camera in hand, ready to click. You'll see photos of plain-Jane backyards like you'd see in any conventional subdivision that have been transformed into waterfront properties designed to make any real estate agent drool, and your imagination take flight.

If you take a long, deep breath and focus your attention, you'll sense the aroma emanating from the water lilies and hear the rustling of cattails and reeds swaying in the soft summer breeze. Keep turning the pages and, as you do, picture an incredibly beautiful water feature and ask yourself how you'd interact with it if it were sitting in your backyard.

LEFT» The purple of the clematis spilling alongside the waterfall, contrasts beautifully with the bright green moss clinging to the rocks.

1

Thousands have lived without love, not one without water.

W.H. ALDEN

Intriguing

FAR LEFT» Longing for a secluded hideaway, a sanctuary in which all the frustrations and disappointments of the day are permanently banned? Mother Nature bids you welcome. LEFT» See the chairs? See the coffee table? See the cascading falls, the meandering stream gliding into the placid pond? Now sit down, prop your feet up on that coffee table, clasp your hands behind your neck, take a long, deep breath, and relax. You deserve it.

5

RIGHT» Kids love ponds. Who needs a video game or a TV when you have a pond?

By any chance, would you say hello to the morning with a steaming cup of coffee and your daily newspaper out by the pond?

Later in the morning, maybe your kids would be lured away from the television set and their video games because the pond and all its critters are so much more intriguing. Would your better half entertain a few friends or enjoy planting a new flower or two late in the afternoon?

RIGHT» Plants, rocks, water, and a weathered log all fall together in this naturally beautiful, ecological work of art. **FAR RIGHT»** The hanging lamp stands out and provides a human touch that contrasts with the otherwise all-natural backdrop.

And when the evening rolls around, the underwater lights automatically switch on, giving you a view of all the activity that goes on within the pond, which is totally different from the things you can see during the day. Invite your friends and neighbors over, light the logs in the fire pit, and soak in the aroma of burning wood and the peaceful sounds of the waterfall, a combination that's impossible to beat whether it's spring, summer, or fall. Now ask yourself, do you feel welcome in the wonderful world of water gardening? Okay then, just come on in and stay awhile.

Everybody needs beauty as well as bread, places to plan in and pray in, where Nature may heal and cheer and give strength to body and soul alike.

JOHN MUIR

CHAPTER 2

AQUATIC ESCAPES

WHEN YOU GO ON VACATION, YOU "ESCAPE" TO ARUBA, JAMAICA,

COSTA RICA, OR THE MEDITERRANEAN. BUT THAT OBSERVATION BEGS THE

QUESTION, "FROM WHAT ARE YOU ESCAPING?"

Let's answer by observing that, despite all the bells and whistles of our modern, technological age, humans still have their roots planted deeply in the bosom of Mother Nature.

The dilemma for most of us is that modern work surrounds us with computers, fax machines, pagers, cell phones, CDs, DVDs, MP3s – a vast array of high-tech "gizmology" that is anything but natural. Star War's R2D2 may be at home in this setting, but for most humans, 40 to 60 hours a week interacting with "robots" constitutes a techno overload from which we long to escape.

How many people do you know who escape to the green grass of the golf course, the towering trees of the closest nature preserve, the infinitely mesmerizing roar of the ocean, or a pleasant conversation with a babbling brook? For many of us, this natural escape is necessary in order to maintain our sanity.

So, let's say hello to the modern hobby of ecosystem water gardening. Let's talk about the little piece of paradise that sits out in your backyard, waiting for you to come home late in the afternoon, kick off your shoes and socks, roll up your pant legs, lower your aching feet into the cool pond water, then kick and splash the water just like you used to do when you were a kid.

You sit listening to the soothing sounds of the water spilling over the rocks in the falls on its way to the pond. You contemplate the colorful koi darting and gliding effortlessly from rock to rock and, occasionally, coming

LEFT» Many water gardening enthusiasts think of their backyard aquatic paradise as a getaway, a hideaway, a secret place accessible only to a few inner-circle friends and family. A gazebo helps perfect that intimate kind of experience.

Contemplate

LEFT» Did your dad or mom ever read you a story about a dark magical forest, with a serene pond highlighted by the rays of sunlight poking through the trees? Behold that pond.

LEFT» With the water flowing, step-by-step over the rocks, surrounded by the greenery, it's impossible to feel stressed or frustrated about anything. Recognize that you have, indeed, escaped. RIGHT» Water gardens make great sit-and-do-nothing spots. Your favorite chair awaits you!

to say hello and nibble on your toes, telling you they'd like a snack.

Taking a long, deep breath, you inhale the aroma of the surrounding plants, flowers, and grasses that make your backyard the envy of your friends and neighbors. And as a butterfly lands on your shoulder and a yellow finch drinks from the stream, you count how many people have told you how amazing your pond is, and how they want one just like it.

RIGHT» The slope of a hill gives you the opportunity to create glorious, multiple waterfalls that tumble their way into the awaiting pond below. A scene like this can take your breath away.

FAR RIGHT» Even on a cloudy day, you can peer deeply into the crystal clear water, see the darting colors with fins, gliding from rock to rock so smoothly, so effortlessly. Can't you just feel the magnetic attraction of this pond?

This is your traveling destination. Your escape. Where you reconnect with your inner child, as the stresses and frustrations slide slowly out of your muscles into the pond, leaving you relaxed and refreshed in a way that you can never be in the techno grind. Just think … you didn't even have to buy a ticket or jump on a plane in order to escape. Congratulations, and welcome to the wonderful world of water gardening.

*Those who
contemplate
the beauty of
the earth find
reserves of
strength that will
endure as long as
life lasts.*

RACHEL CARSON

*The main
purpose of a
garden is to give
its owner the
best and highest
kind of earthly
pleasure.*

GERTRUDE JEKYLL

ABOVE» Some people think they don't have room for a pond, but small ponds and water features can be tucked into almost any size yard. Even under the deck of a home with no yard makes a great place for a pond. **LEFT»** Green is almost always the color of Mother Nature's canvas. Here, she contrasts it marvelously with the red of an aging shed, the gray, blue, and pink of surrounding rocks, the dark silhouette of a maple tree, the multicolored flowers, and the small, inadvertent statue that reveals a human accent.

15

FAR RIGHT» It's amazing just how closely you can bring a pond and a house together. This pond is so close to the deck that you could easily sit down and dangle your feet into the pond, or feed the fish. **RIGHT»** For most enthusiasts, water gardening is all about the opportunity to relax and enjoy life. Picture yourself sitting in this swing, with or without a friend, just listening to the sounds of Mother Nature in the stillness of your own magnificent water feature.

16

*For me, a
landscape does
not exist in its
own right, since
its appearance
changes at every
moment, but
the surrounding
atmosphere
brings it to life
— the light and
the air, which
vary continually.
For me, it is only
the surrounding
atmosphere,
which gives
subjects their
true value.*

CLAUDE MONET

ABOVE» How about
a HIGH FIVE for the
waterfalls?
FAR LEFT» A peaceful
evening spent by the
pond is made pos-
sible by landscape
and pond lighting.

Escape

3
PEOPLE
& PONDS

REMEMBER WHEN YOUR NEIGHBORS WEREN'T ALWAYS SO ...

NEIGHBORLY? IT'S BEEN A LONG TIME, HASN'T IT? IN FACT, IF YOU REALLY
TRACK HOW LONG IT'S BEEN, YOU MIGHT FIND YOURSELF THINKING BACK
to a couple of summers ago. You know, the summer you got your water
garden. Bingo!

It's true; people seem to be drawn to ponds. Once you put one in,
neighbors from three doors away suddenly come down to introduce themselves and, before you know it, you're having the first block party in your
own backyard. For generations, people have been drawn to water – from the
canals that twist and turn throughout Venice, to the beachside mansions of
movie stars.

Water, whether it's in the form of a manmade creation or Mother Nature's own work, is a part of us. Our bodies are made up of about 60 percent
water and we need water to survive. It's an attraction that we'll never be able
to resist.

But that's not why you got your pond. You just wanted a beautiful water
garden in your very own backyard, and when it happened to earn you a few
more friends around town, it was an added bonus. And your kids ... oh, how
your kids enjoy the cool moving stream and gushing waterfall! They could sit
for hours and watch the fish swim back and forth under your bridge. Time in
front of the television is easily traded for a chance to feed the hungry little
koi as they nibble on fingers and toes in hopes of grasping that one pellet of
food from the clutched hand of your little angel.

LEFT» Don't be
surprised if your
pond attracts curious
visitors, anxious to
investigate
and explore.

25

In all things of
nature there is
something of the
marvelous.

Aristotle

Captivate

RIGHT» Hunting for new and exciting creatures becomes even more of a child's favorite pastime when water is introduced to your yard. **FAR RIGHT»** Don't be afraid to let your child's imagination run wild in the pond.

While you watch the children marvel at the pond and all its amazing glory, you can't help but think about the "big kid" fun that will be going on later that night. Once the sun sets, it's just the grownups, dining on your backyard patio with the underwater lights of the pond reflecting up through the waterfall, casting a dim light on the smiling faces of your friends. And wine always tastes better when accompanied by the sights and sounds of pure beauty. Or what about that hot cup of coffee or cocoa in the cold

LEFT» Feeding your aquatic pets becomes a favorite time of day. You can even train them to come to the same spot every day for feeding time.

Keeping in touch with childhood memories keeps us believing in life's simplest pleasures like a rainy afternoon, a swing set, and a giant puddle to play in.

Chrissy Ogden

FAR LEFT» Everyone needs a little quiet time, complete with a peaceful water garden. LEFT» Fast friends and new acquaintances are made by the pond.

winter months, with a view from your living room of the icy creations forming on the waterfall? Now there's a conversation piece for a room full of old and new friends.

Every day, water gardens fill the people that surround them with joy, whether it's the little boy who drops his book bag off at the door and runs to see the frog that's made its home in the brush alongside the pond, or the woman escaping from the 9-to-5 grind in favor of a little therapeutic gardening. Oh, how great it is!

ABOVE» Teaching your children to respect wildlife is a lesson that will stay with them forever. FAR RIGHT» Escape from a hectic 9-to-5 workday next to your water garden, and the stresses of the day will melt away. RIGHT» It might be scary at first, but it's fun to let your fish take a nibble.

The earth
laughs in flowers.

RALPH WALDO
EMERSON

Relaxation

FAR LEFT» Long conversations with old friends are always memorable next to a beautiful pond setting. LEFT» A quiet reading place is always available at a moment's notice.

35

RIGHT» Plan a picnic next to your pond and enjoy the sights and sounds of the natural surroundings.

ABOVE» Who needs video games and television when you've got a live, after-school water show every day? **RIGHT**» Let your children name their fish. After all, they are pets with personality.

The joy of looking and comprehending is nature's most beautiful gift.

ALBERT EINSTEIN

Adopt the pace of nature: her secret is patience.

RALPH WALDO EMERSON

Reflect

38

CHAPTER 4

WATERFALLS
& STREAMS

IMAGINE YOURSELF LYING IN YOUR COZY BED, DREAMING THE MOST
WONDERFUL DREAM ABOUT YOUR ADVENTURES AS A CHILD – WHEN YOU
FROLICKED THROUGH THE WOODS IN YOUR GRANDPARENTS' BACKYARD. THE
grass is wet on your feet with the cool morning dew and birds are flittering
in front of you, collecting twigs and other materials to build a new home. The
dream is so real that you can actually hear the babbling brook, laughing and
gurgling, almost singing in your ear.

You slowly awaken from your slumber only to realize that the sounds of
that babbling brook are still echoing, and you remember the greatest invest-
ment you've ever made as you stroll over to the open window and look down
upon your aquatic backyard paradise. You have a gorgeous waterfall with a
flowing stream dropping into the pond below. Aren't you lucky?

Waterfalls and streams certainly are beautiful, serving as the focal points
of the pond, and perhaps your entire landscape. In fact, sometimes people are
so enamored with waterfalls and streams that they couldn't care less whether
the pond even exists. But how can you have both of those attractions without
a pond? It's called a Pondless® Waterfall, a water gardening marvel that eliminates the maintenance of a pond, as the waterfall and stream empty into a
basin of gravel. It couldn't be more beautiful – or more simple.

Ah, to live the life of the water … flowing over the waterfalls, dashing
through the stream … splashing, darting, and dipping the entire way. Along
the way, you may encounter some smooth pebbles, uncovering a softer side
of the stream, or perhaps you'll bump into the resident rebel of the group …

LEFT» There's nothing
like a beautiful wa-
terfall to accent your
pond. In fact, it can
make or break your
whole landscape!
ABOVE» A Pondless®
Waterfall is perfect
for the water garden
enthusiast who has
a small and limited
space in which to
work, and it almost
totally eliminates
any maintenance or
liability concerns.

RIGHT» The bigger the drop, the better – especially when there's plenty of water flowing over the falls. **FAR RIGHT»** An up-close and personal view of this stream reveals the intricate twists and turns of the design.

46

way to provide the necessary effect of the water splashing down. And your stream, whether it's twisting and turning or straight and narrow, gives your pond more character and defines your whole backyard.

So the next time you wake up from your good night's rest and look out at the gorgeous accents of your pond, remember how lucky you are to have brought the babbling brook of your childhood to your own backyard. Isn't it great to be a water gardener?

*If there is magic
on the planet,
it is contained
in the water.*

LOREN EISELEY

49

Mesmerize

FAR LEFT» There's something to be said for leaving a little moss on the rocks when it creates this beautiful scene. LEFT» Looking to spice up the waterfall and stream a bit? Try placing a large stone in the middle to direct water either way.

50

ABOVE» Using worn wood and native stone to accent your stream adds a little something extra and makes it feel like it belongs in the space.

RIGHT» It's always good to line a long, winding stream with foliage of all kinds. Go ahead and experiment!

Those who dwell among the beauties and mysteries of the earth are never alone or weary of life.

RACHEL CARSON

63

FAR LEFT» Pond enthusiasts love dragonflies for their unique beauty and their endless appetite for mosquitoes, of which they may eat many times their own body weight each day.
LEFT» Plants and fish do their parts in helping to keep your ecosystem pond clean and clear but, more importantly, they provide us with beauty and grace.

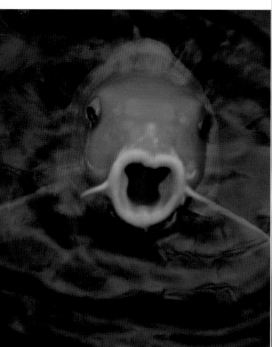

66

RIGHT» Fish and
flowers, yellow and
red, dark and light …
it's in all the contrasts
that pondering finds
its characteristic
uniqueness. It's also
where you can find
your own uniqueness
at the very same
time.

Let us permit nature to have her way. She understands her business better than we do.

MICHEL DE MONTAIGNE

CHAPTER 6

AQUATIC PLANTS

SURE YOU HAVE A WATER GARDEN THAT YOU LOOK OUT AT AND

ADMIRE, BUT ARE YOU TRULY A WATER "GARDENER"? ARE YOU THE TYPE OF

PERSON WHO DONS WADERS AND SHUFFLES OUT TO THE MIDDLE OF THE

pond to place a fertilizer tab in their precious tropical water lilies?

One of the greatest things about having that puddle of beauty in your

backyard is the fact that you can expand your gardening pallet to include

aquatic plants. Aquatic plants ... a whole new world of leaves, petals, and

roots ready to be explored.

Soon you're in the local garden center, perusing the plants and deciding

which ones to add to your water garden. Will you choose the jewel of the

pond ... the water lily? With beautiful, vibrant colors that dot the surface of

your water garden, perhaps hardy varieties like Joey Tomocik, Mayla, or Colo-

rado will tickle your fancy. Then there are the tropicals, with fragrant flowers

that stand above the water, awaiting your stolen glances. Night-bloomers are

often a good choice, since they're always there to greet you after a long day

of work. So many choices!

A favorite of every water gardener is the lotus, the king of the pond. Its

huge leaves and giant flowers are breathtaking and almost addicting. Even

neophyte gardeners can grow the lotus, since it is at home in anything from a

3-acre pond to a small whiskey barrel.

Maybe you're not the type of pond lover who revels in the gardening experi-

ence. You still can't keep yourself from floating a lily into your pond or strategically

placing water hyacinth near your waterfall, all to help keep your pond healthy and

LEFT» There are
moments in the
pond world when
it seems like all
life forms are
simultaneously
erupting into
existence and color.

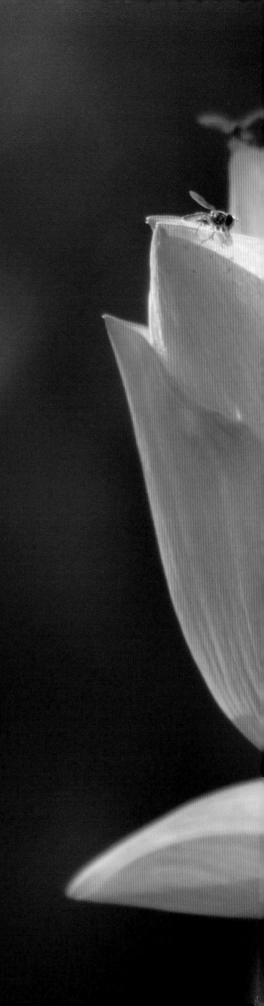

RIGHT» From pot to gorgeous flower, the transformation of a lotus is breathtaking, and all its stages interesting.
FAR RIGHT» This statuesque lotus is alive with color, and serves as a pretty nice resting place for passing insects.

clean. After all, clear, healthy, all-natural ecosystem ponds depend on plants to keep everything balanced.

The truth is, plants help rid your water garden of the nutrients that feed ugly green algae. No nutrients ... no algae. Yes, the aquatic plants in your backyard water garden are part of a home biology class, perfect for children looking to learn more about the environment and the world around them. Aquatic plants certainly are amazing, aren't they?

*Study nature,
love nature, stay
close to nature.
It will never fail
you.*

Frank Lloyd Wright

Meditate

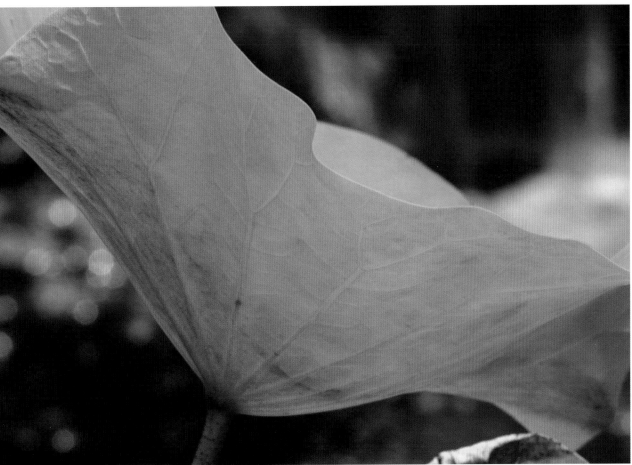

FAR LEFT» A clematis tumbles down the side of the waterfall, and its blue flowers peek out from behind a graceful white water lily.
LEFT» The grand nature of a lotus leaf is truly spectacular.

73

RIGHT» The soft lavender color of this lily complements the surface of any pond.

But plants don't just serve a biological purpose in the pond. They also provide food, shelter, and much-needed shade for the critters that come to visit your pond every day. Go ahead and look out your window at your aquatic plants and watch the insects darting from petal to petal, continuing the circle of life by fertilizing and feeding. What would your pond do without plants ... beautiful, functional plants? And you only bought them because you thought they were good looking. Smart guess!

74

RIGHT» Tropical water
lilies are distinctive
because the flowers
sit above the water.
FAR RIGHT» When
creating a scenic and
interesting pond-
scape, the colorful
plants around a water
garden are just as
important as the
aquatic plants in it.

Fascinate

Everywhere water is a thing of beauty gleaming in the dewdrop, singing in the summer rain.

John Ballantine Gough

77

LEFT» Water lilies look especially graceful when they balance droplets of water on their fragile petals. ABOVE» Add a bit of color to your water garden with a splash of pink!

Enchant

Nature does not hurry, yet everything is accomplished.

LAO TZU

*If we had no
winter, the spring
would not be so
pleasant.*

ANNE BRADSTREET

CHAPTER

7

SEASONS CHANGE

IF THERE IS ONLY ONE CONSTANT IN NATURE, IT'S THAT EVERYTHING

IS CONSTANTLY CHANGING – EVERYTHING IS EVOLVING ALL THE TIME.

MOTHER NATURE NEVER RESTS, SHE NEVER GETS TIRED. THE EARTH KEEPS

right on spinning, the sun keeps right on revolving, and summer turns into fall,

fall into winter, winter into spring, and spring into summer – just like clockwork,

year after year. That's the nature of Mother Nature. One of the most wonderful

ways to fully appreciate this constant change is by having a water garden in

your backyard.

During the summer, the water garden is at its most soothing, when eve-

ning breezes cool a steamy evening, and the lights in the evening pond are

most romantic. The colors of the pondscape are the brightest and critters are

most likely to stop in to pay a visit. And in the heat of a summer afternoon,

the kids can cool off in the pond with good, clean, educational fun. Mean-

while, the sounds of the waterfall are the most relaxing. Is there a better time

of the year to be a pond lover? Probably not.

In the autumn, as leaves start turning deep shades of red, orange, and yel-

low, you see their reflection in the light ripple of your pond. There's a little chill

in the air, but the flames in your pondside fire pit warm you, while the trickling

sound of the nearby waterfall relaxes you. You relish the last chance to enjoy

your water garden before winter sets in. It's truly a magical experience. Is there

a better time of the year to be a pond lover? Probably not.

In the winter, the view from inside your warm, toasty home reveals

that your once liquid, flowing waterfall has turned into the most amazingly

LEFT» This photo could have been snapped in Savannah, Georgia or Billings, Montana. But one thing is for sure, the petals on the tree tell you that it's spring-time by the pond. **ABOVE»** When travel-ing from springtime into summer, it's always handy to have a footbridge to cross over.

Dream

A thing of beauty
is a joy forever:
Its loveliness
increases; it will
never pass into
nothingness.

JOHN KEATS

Spellbound

FAR LEFT» An up-close look at a winter waterfall reveals the sheer colors of winter. Be careful if you get too close – your tongue can still stick to the ice. **LEFT»** The waterfall continues to fall but in the winter, Mother Nature changes the scenery of your water garden. Ice and snow sculptures begin to form as the new fallen snow collects on the surrounding landscape.

RIGHT» The grip of Jack Frost turns this waterfall into a jagged, icy creation with its own special beauty.

beautiful ice sculpture. As the pond's surface slowly turns to ice, the blanket of new-fallen snow covers the pond waiting below. Is there a better time of the year to be a pond lover? Yes, there is. But the winter pond still has a beauty all its own.

Then there is spring. After months of cold, indoor living, spring can easily be the most magical time of the year around the pond. Everything is springing back to life at once. The plants around the pond peek out from

FAR RIGHT» Slopes with steps, trees, lights, plants, and water all blend together to form an enchanting late afternoon composition that helps bring out the deep, natural colors surrounding the pond. **RIGHT AND LOWER RIGHT»** The contrast of two different seasons shows this pond with a shimmering, wintery blanket of snow and the cheerful green of summer.

under their protective cover of autumn leaves and snow as they search for the warmth of the spring sunshine. Their colors can brighten up any rainy spring day, and the colorful fish that have been hibernating through winter are waking up as well. Is there a better time of the year to be a pond lover? Most definitely not!

TOP» Even on a cold and dreary winter day, the presence of a waterfall spilling into a pond below creates movement, interest, and intrigue.

Autumn is a second spring when every leaf is a flower.

ALBERT CAMUS

To everything,
turn, turn, turn.
There is a season,
turn, turn, turn.
And a time to
every purpose
under heaven …

PETE SEEGER

CHAPTER

8

A HOBBY
FOR LIFE

LEFT» A small backyard is transformed by a tranquil pond, creating a peaceful and romantic place to relax and "get away."

WHETHER YOU'RE A WEEKDAY WORK ADDICT SEEKING SOLACE ON
WEEKENDS NEXT TO YOUR RELAXING BACKYARD PARADISE, OR AN AVID
GARDENER LOOKING TO ADD A LITTLE WATER TO YOUR PLANT COLLECTION,
ponds truly are a blessing.

No one but Mother Nature herself can duplicate the beautiful sights and
sounds that emanate from these brilliant works of art, and no two water gardens
are ever the same. Surrounded by landscaping of all shapes and sizes, some will
have distinctive color palettes, while others are wild with diversity. A green hue of
moss collecting on rocks near the side of the water garden may be present in some
ponds, while others may be shielded by the delicate leaves of the lotus or water lily.

And the waterfalls take your breath away each and every time you look at
them, with their draping water hyacinths and long, flowing streams. How can
anyone resist dipping their toes into a rushing stream on a hot summer day?
Or what about the cool and relaxing pond below, still with a tranquility that
can only be broken by a hungry koi coming up for a nibble of food?

Even when the weather turns brisk, simply looking at the pond and its
delicate ecosystem can relieve the stresses of even the most unbearable
day. The solitary cattail that is holding on until the cold weather hits, the
water lily that huddles next to the boulders for warmth, or even the fish
lurking near the bottom of the pond awaiting hibernation is not sad, but a
gentle reminder that everything will live and bloom again.

Water gardening is a hobby that can span a lifetime, from generation to generation. Its look may change from year to year as the newest

FAR LEFT» Floating aquatics, like these water lettuce, play a critical role in keeping your pond naturally balanced and minimizing the required maintenance time and effort. They're also naturally beautiful. **LEFT»** Some folks contend that we could save an entire generation of kids by giving them all easy access to a pond. You could call it early childhood inspiration.

95

RIGHT» Bridges connect, overcome, and present an opportunity to view your pond from an entirely unique perspective. Yes, bridges and ponds almost always complement one another.

varieties of water lilies make their way to the surface of your pond, and it may even be expanded or remodeled a few times over, but it's still a pond … your pond. Your children will grow to play in it and learn from it. Together you will spend hours and hours sitting beside it as the water garden serves as your mini-vacation from the rest of the world.

You will entertain by the pond, exchange views by the pond, and sit down to family meals by the pond. You

RIGHT» Directionality plays a role in the appeal of any pond. Some things, like these lily pads for example, are flat and horizontal. Others, like the canna and umbrella palm, are tall and vertical. While still others crisscross, run over, under, and around, all in an effort to naturalize the pond and seduce the human eye. **FAR RIGHT»** Reflections are also part and parcel of ponds. The pond surface reflects the surrounding plants and the sky. The waterfalls glisten as they reflect the sunlight. Now take a little time to reflect on your own thoughts. In the end, that's what pondering is all about.

Aquatic Plants are Mother Nature's true filters. Plants are great for adding character to a pond by providing color and texture, but from a filtration perspective, they're second to none. Thriving from the excess nutrients in a pond and depriving algae of its food source, the proper coverage of aquatic plants in a water garden is critical for the overall health of the ecosystem.

will talk to friends by the pond, make friends by the pond, and your pond will invite new people to become friends.

The opportunities are endless when you've been bitten by the water gardening bug. The only thing left to do now is pass on your love of gardening to someone else – someone who you can share stories, ideas, and even plants with. More plants? Why didn't you think of getting your friends involved sooner? Happy Pondering!

A Circulation System is really just a fancy term for Pumps and Plumbing. The proper size pump and pipe diameter are extremely important for the aesthetics of a water feature, but more importantly, an efficient circulation system will keep the water moving and provide the necessary oxygen levels for healthy fish and plants.

The Ecosystem Pond

There are five key ingredients to creating a natural, low-maintenance ecosystem pond in your backyard.

- Aquatic Plants
- Circulation System
- Filtration System (BIOFALLS® filter and skimmer)
- Fish
- Rocks, Gravel, and Bacteria

But that's not all. A good ecosystem also contains other integral elements.

Fish are an integral part of any pond ecosystem. Unfortunately, fish are often seen as being the cause of a maintenance nightmare. Contrary to popular belief, fish actually reduce pond maintenance by grazing on string algae and bottom feeding from the pond floor.

Plant pockets around six inches deep and filled with soil, promote health in plant development by allowing the roots to spread through surrounding gravel, unlike containerized plants, which can quickly become root-bound.

A strong, **45-mil EPDM liner** is the best choice for most pond installations. Unlike concrete, it is easy and inexpensive to install and won't crack. When covered with stone, it has a 40-year life expectancy. If a leak ever were to occur, a simple inner-tube patch kit can make it as good as new.

A woven, needle-punched underlayment forms a soft padding for the liner. Unlike newspapers, it's quick to install. Unlike sand, it completely covers the vertical areas of the pond shelves.

Rocks, Gravel, and Bacteria have been controversial elements in water gardening for many years. Many enthusiasts have steered away from them out of fear that they will create additional maintenance. Gravel, unlike a smooth pond liner, not only protects pond liners from UV light degradation, but also provides tremendous surface area for beneficial bacteria to break down excess nutrients in the water and dissolved organic debris on the pond floor. Anaerobic "pond sludge" is therefore decreased naturally – the way nature intended it to be. Plus, a gravel bottom looks far more natural and is safer to walk on than an exposed, slippery rubber liner.

A proper **Filtration System** includes the use of both a BIOFALLS® filter and a skimmer. A BIOFALLS® filter provides surface area for beneficial bacteria to colonize and help remove excess nutrients from the water. A skimmer will not only pre-filter the water and house the pump, but will also skim debris from the water's surface to prevent the decomposition of organic materials on the pond floor.

When you put your hand in a flowing stream, you touch the last that has gone before and the first of what is still to come.

LEONARDO DA VINCI

Transformations

There's a difference between a beautiful home and a spectacularly beautiful home. In this instance, the waterfall and the meandering stream work together to spell out SPECTACULAR!

How often is it that a garden, beautiful though it may be, will seem sad and dreary and lacking in one of its most gracious features, if it has no water?

Pierre Husson

103

Have you ever seen a yard transformed from colorless to colorful in the blink of an eye? In eight to 10 hours, this dull backyard was transformed to intriguing and appealing. Yes, it really is all about water gardening.

Transformations

The proverbial gazebo is stately and interesting sitting all by itself in a green grass backyard. But placing it alongside a lush and colorful water garden makes it stand out and attract even more.

Every backyard can provide a wonderful home for a beautiful water garden. But a yard with a hill is any pond builder's special dream, presenting rich opportunities for creativity that truly allows the imagination to take flight.

RESOURCES

DIVE INTO THE WORLD OF WATER GARDENING WITH *THE ECOSYSTEM POND*, A NEW BOOK FROM THE PUBLISHERS OF *WATER GARDEN LIFESTYLES*. *THE ECOSYSTEM POND* IS A FULL-COLOR, GLOSSY MASTERPIECE THAT PREACHES THE WONDERS OF water gardening the all-natural way. With tons of inspiring photographs and loads of information, this book is a must-have for anyone that has or is looking to get a pond of their own. *The Ecosystem Pond* covers topics from fish and plants to maintenance and troubleshooting, giving everyone an in-depth look at the world of ponds. *The Ecosystem Pond* will motivate and inspire you to add on to your own pond or landscaping work. Ask your local water garden retailer for *The Ecosystem Pond*, and get ready to let your imagination run wild!

Aquascape Lifestyles magazine is your source for everything pond-related. From stories about people just like you to fun articles about what you can do around your pond, *Aquascape Lifestyles* has it covered. Browse the gorgeous photographs, taken by professionals and people just like you, and take in the words of the best garden writers in the country. Learn more about aquatic plants and fish, or completely redesign your pond based on your favorite article … you'll find all kinds of ideas in this quarterly publication. The money obtained through 1 and 2 year subscriptions supports the North American Water Garden Society (NAWGS). For more information and a free sample copy, log on to **www.aquascapelifestyles.com** or call 877-206-7035 and ask for promotion code NTCB01.

The North American Water Garden Society (NAWGS) is a non-profit organization of pond lovers, dedicated to the enjoyment, education, promotion, and protection of the water gardening hobby. With chapters throughout North America, NAWGS encourages water gardeners everywhere to share their thoughts, ideas, and questions at scheduled meetings throughout the year. With their annual NAWGS membership, pond lovers also receive a 1-year subscription to *Aquascape Lifestyles* magazine, in which NAWGS publishes a quarterly newsletter. Get discounts on pond products and services, attend meetings locally and nationally, meet fellow water gardeners, and learn more about the hobby with NAWGS! For more information or to become a member of NAWGS, log on to **www.nawgs.org** or call 877-206-7035.

If you are looking to put in a water feature or to upgrade the one you already have in your backyard, but are having a hard time finding a reliable, professional water garden installer, look for the Certified Aquascape Contractor logo! A Certified Aquascape Contractor (CAC) installs water features using the "ecosystem" method and Aquascape Designs' products. For a listing of CACs in your area, log on to **www.aquascapedesigns.com/contractor/index.php**.

If you've been searching for other people who are just as pond-crazy as you are, you should check out the Aquascape Designs Message Boards at **www.aquascapedesigns.com**. There, you'll find a whole web community of people just like you who are posting ideas, looking for answers, or are just plain chatting about their ponds, and the rest of their backyards.

CONTRIBUTORS

COVER PHOTO BY SPALLEK HEIKO

ALCALA, TONY *Pg 4, 7, 20, 21 (below), 28 (below), 42*

AQUASCAPE DESIGNS FILE PHOTO
Pg VII, VIII, IX, 9-10, 11 (bottom), 12 (top and bottom), 15, 17, 21 (top), 31 (below), 32 (top), 33, 41, 45 (bottom), 46 (top), 55, 74 (right), 75, 78-79, 83, 85 (top), 88 (bottom), 89, 100-103

BUSH, TODD *Pg 11 (top), 49 (right)*

CHERMANSKY, STEPHEN *Pg 50 (left)*

DAVIS, SCOTT AND ANNE *Pg 36, 59 (top), 85 (bottom), 96 (top)*

DECK AND PATIO COMPANY *Pg 1, 86 (top and bottom), 90, 98*

EXOTIC AQUATICS *Pg 104*

FINNELL, ROBIN *Pg 58*

GAIBLER, DENNIS *Pg 94*

GARTON, ABIGAIL *Pg 31 (top)*

HAGEN, PHIL *Pg 64 (left)*

HANKS, MARTIN *Pg 24, 72*

HEIKO, SPALLEK *Cover, Pg 6 (top)*

HUGHES, SCOTT *Pg 0, 6 (bottom), 8, 13-14, 18, 22, 26, 34, 37, 40, 44, 45 (top), 49 (left), 54, 56 (right), 59 (bottom), 60 (bottom), 61-63, 64 (right), 66 (right), 69-71, 73 (top), 74 (left), 76, 82, 84, 88 (top)*

LANGLEY, BECKY *Pg 16 (bottom)*

LONGHORN LANDSCAPING *Pg 87*

MACDONALD, MIKE *Pg 56 (left), 92*

O'DANIEL, LEANE *Pg 38*

PASTOR, MARK *Pg 5 (top), 50 (right), 53, 68*

PERRY, DON *Pg 75*

PLANTENANCE *Pg 95 (bottom)*

PONDSAWAY *Pg 93*

PREMIER PONDS *Pg 23, 98*

REUTIMANN, DAN *Pg 5 (bottom), 95 (top)*

RICHERT, BILL *Pg 77, 39, 96 (bottom)*

RUEL, MARY *Pg 81*

SILER, LYNNE *Pg 16 (top), 30, 48*

STUDLEY, KERRIE *Pg 28 (top), 29, 32 (bottom)*

TRANQUIL WATER GARDENS *Pg 80*

WEMCO *Pg 3, 46 (bottom)*

WIERZBICKI, NANCY *Pg 25, 35 (top)*

WOODLAND WATER GARDENS *Pg 105*